# Im Reich der urigen Buchen
# In the kingdom of quaint beeches

Manfred Delpho & Wolfgang Lübcke

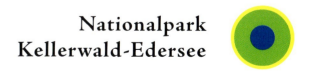

# Impressum / Imprint

*Die Autoren / The authors:*

**Manfred Delpho** Zum Fotografieren ist Manfred Delpho, geboren am 7.7.1948 in Kassel, über die Naturschutzarbeit beim NABU gekommen. Hier entdeckte er vor über 20 Jahren seine Liebe und sein Talent zur Naturfotografie. Sein Hobby hat er zum Beruf gemacht. In vielen Büchern und Magazinen werden seine Fotos veröffentlicht. Zwei Bildbände „Naturerlebnis Nordhessen" sind bisher erschienen. Er hat national und international viele bedeutende Fotopreise gewonnen. Im Jahr 2002 wurde er von der Gesellschaft Deutscher Tierfotografen zum „Naturfotograf des Jahres" gewählt. Einen kleinen Einblick in seine fotografische Arbeit bekommt man auf der Webseite www.delpho.de.

**Manfred Delpho**, born in Kassel on 7th July 1948, found his interest in photography through his nature conservation work with the NABU (Nature Conservation Confederation Germany) and discovered his love and his talent for nature photography 20 years ago. He turned his hobby into a profession. His photographs are published in many books and magazines. Two volumes of photographs entitled "Naturerlebnis Nordhessen" ("Experience the Nature of Northern Hessen") have been published so far. He has won many distinguished prizes, both national and international, for his photographs. In 2002 he was elected „Nature Photographer of the Year" by the Gesellschaft Deutscher Tierphotographen (Society of German Animal Photographers). A small insight into his photographic work can be gained from his website www.delpho.de.

**Wolfgang Lübcke** wurde am 2.12.1941 in Parchim / Mecklenburg geboren. Nach dem Abitur in Bad Wildungen studierte er die Fächer Biologie und Deutsch. Der Oberstudiendirektor a. D. war Leiter des Studienseminars für Gymnasien in Kassel. Seit seinem elften Lebensjahr engagiert er sich ehrenamtlich im Naturschutz. Er ist langjähriger Vorsitzender des NABU Edertal, war Kreisvorsitzender des NABU Waldeck-Frankenberg, Mitglied des Landesvorstandes der HGON und des Landesnaturschutzbeirats. Aus seiner Feder stammen zahlreiche natur- und heimatkundliche Publikationen. Er ist Schriftleiter der „Vogelkundlichen Hefte Edertal" und der Reihe „Naturschutz in Waldeck-Frankenberg".

**Wolfgang Lübcke** was born in Parchim / Mecklenburg on 2nd December 1941. After having completed his Final Examinations in Bad Wildungen, he took on a course of studies in Biology and German. The principal (retired) was head of the studies seminar for grammar schools in Kassel. He has been volunteering his time to nature conservation work since the age of 11. He is the longstanding chairman of the NABU Edertal, was district chairman of the NABU Waldeck-Frankenberg district, member of the state board of directors of the HGON (Hesse Society of Ornithology and Nature Conservation) and of the state advisory council for nature conservation. He has penned many publications in the fields of natural and local history. He is the editor of „Vogelkundliche Hefte Edertal" (Edertal Ornithology Journal) and of the series „Naturschutz in Waldeck-Frankenberg" (Nature conservation in Waldeck-Frankenberg).

**Herausgeber:**
Nationalpark Kellerwald-Edersee
Laustraße 8, 34537 Bad Wildungen
Telefon: 0049. (0) 5621 75249-0
Fax: 0049. (0) 5621-19
E-Mail: info@nationalpark-kellerwald-edersee.de
www.nationalpark-kellerwald-edersee.de

NABU-Landesverband-Hessen
Geschäftsstelle
Friedensstr. 26, 35578 Wetzlar
Telefon: 0049. (0) 6441 67904-0
Fax: 0049. (0) 6441 67904-29
E-Mail: nabu.hessen@t-online.de

**Fotos:** Manfred Delpho
**Texte:** Wolfgang Lübcke
**Übersetzung:** Birgit Nizami

**Druck:**
Strube OHG, 34587 Felsberg

**Gestaltung und Vertrieb:**
cognitio Verlag
Westendstraße 23, 34305 Niedenstein
Telefon: 0049. (0) 5624 925024
Fax: 0049. (0) 5624 8170
E-Mail: info@cognitio.de, www.cognitio.de

**ISBN 978-3-932583-18-6**

© 2006 cognitio
Das Werk einschließlich aller seiner Teile ist urheberrechtlich geschützt. Jede Verwertung außerhalb der engen Grenzen des Urheberrechtsgesetzes ist ohne Zustimmung des Herausgebers und des Verlags unzulässig und strafbar. Das gilt insbesondere für Vervielfältigungen, Übersetzungen, Mikroverfilmungen und die Einspeicherung und Verarbeitung in elektronischen Systemen.

**Gefördert von** der Stiftung Hessischer Naturschutz

# Vorwort / Foreword

**Wilhelm Dietzel**
(Staatsminister)

Hessen ist mit einem Anteil von 42 % der Landesfläche ein sehr waldreiches Land. Hessen ist zudem mit 41 % der Waldfläche das Land der Baumart Buche. Wir Hessen sind stolz darauf, im Herzen von Deutschland große und wertvolle Buchenwälder als Naturgut zu haben. Diesem Naturgut fühlen wir uns verpflichtet, es bildet unsere Lebensgrundlage und bedeutet für uns Heimat. Unsere Buchenwälder liefern uns Holz, den ökologischsten aller Roh- und Werkstoffe.

Eine nachhaltige, pflegliche und naturnahe Waldbewirtschaftung unserer Forstleute war und bleibt der Garant für eine naturverträgliche Waldbewirtschaftung.

Brauchen wir einen Nationalpark in Hessen?
Ja, wir brauchen ihn!
In der Region Kellerwald-Edersee befindet sich der größte Hainsimsen-Buchenwaldkomplex Mitteleuropas. Wir haben im Herbst 2004 diese wunderbare Landschaft der urigen Buchenwälder, der Mittelgebirgshöhen, der natürlichen Bachtäler und Seen auf einer Fläche von 57 km² zum Nationalpark erklärt. Wir möchten dieses für Hessen typische Ökosystem in seiner Ursprünglichkeit bewahren.

Lassen Sie sich ein auf das „Abenteuer Wildnis" – im Nationalpark erleben Sie „Natur pur"!
Der vorliegende Bildband entführt Sie in „das Reich der urigen Buchen". Die hervorragenden Naturaufnahmen werden Sie begeistern und Ihre Sehnsucht wecken, die Schönheit unserer Natur selbst zu erleben.
Tauchen Sie ein in das „Buchenmeer", besuchen Sie unseren Nationalpark und die Region Kellerwald-Edersee.

With a share of 42 % of the Land's surface, Hessen is a densely wooded Land. Hessen is also the Land of the beech trees which cover 41 % of the forest's surface. We Hessians are proud to have extensive and valuable beech groves as natural heritage in the heart of Germany. It is to this natural heritage that we feel committed. It forms the basis of our lives and it means home to us. Our beech groves provide wood, the most ecological of all raw and basic materials.

A lasting careful and near-natural forest cultivation of our forest officials was and remains the guarantee for ecologically sound forest cultivation.

Do we need a national park in Hessen?
Yes, we need one!
The largest Luzulo-Fagetum beech grove complex of central Europe is located in the Kellerwald-Edersee region. This beautiful landscape of quaint beech groves, low mountain ranges, natural creek valleys and lakes in an area of 57 km² was declared national park by us in autumn 2004. We would like to protect this ecosystem which is typical of Hessen in its nativeness.

Get involved with the „adventure in the wilderness" – in the national park you will experience „true nature"!
This illustrated book will whisk you away into the „kingdom of quaint beeches". These superb nature photographs will inspire you and rouse your desire for experiencing the beauty of our nature yourself.
Dive into the „sea of beeches", visit our national park and the Kellerwald-Edersee region.

# Vorwort / Foreword

Peter Gaffert
(Leiter Nationalparkamt
Kellerwald-Edersee)

Gute Gedanken sind oft ihrer Zeit weit voraus. Anders ist es wohl nicht zu verstehen, dass die Idee zum Nationalpark Kellerwald-Edersee fast 20 Jahre brauchte, um Realität zu werden.
Doch seit drei Jahren bereichert er die internationale Familie der Nationalparks in aller Welt. Zweifellos zählt er zu den kleinsten Nationalparken, seine einzigartige Naturausstattung, sein Artenreichtum und seine Ursprünglichkeit auf unzerschnittener Fläche machen ihn jedoch zu etwas besonders Wertvollem.
Werden und Vergehen, der Jahrmillionen alte Zyklus allen Lebens, läuft vor unseren Augen ab. Täglich. Überall. Und wir sind selbst Teil dieses Prozesses. Voller Bewunderung sind wir beim Anblick uralter Bäume, fasziniert von der Urkraft der Natur, sich stets selbst am Leben zu erhalten. Allein der Begriff Nationalpark erzeugt bei vielen Sehnsucht nach unberührter Natur. Bei uns liegt sie vor der Haustür. Im Nationalpark Kellerwald-Edersee geht der Wald seinen eigenen Weg, nicht planbar und immer wieder überraschend. Er zeigt Vergänglichkeit und Werden, oft auf engstem Raum, offenbart Eigenständigkeit, unvorstellbare Kraft, Vielfalt und Schönheit. Wenn wir eintauchen in diesen Wald, in das Reich der urigen Buchen, stehen wir all diesen Facetten staunend, vielleicht auch erschrocken oder verunsichert gegenüber. Doch wenn wir es zulassen, unsere Sinne schärfen, dann ergreift uns die Faszination Wildnis.
Dieses Buch will Sie einladen, die wieder entstehende Waldwildnis im Nationalpark zu entdecken. Freuen Sie sich auf eine spannende Entdeckungsreise durch einen der letzten ursprünglichen Buchenwälder Europas. Die brillanten Fotos und Beschreibungen machen diesen Bildband zur exklusiven Visitenkarte einer einzigartigen Landschaft Nordhessens.

Good thoughts are often ahead of their times. It cannot be seen otherwise that the concept of the Kellerwald-Edersee National Park took 20 years to become reality. For three years now it has however been a part of the international family of national parks the world over. It is definitely one of the smallest national parks but its unique natural equipment, its species richness and its nativeness in a coherent area make it something invaluable.
Growth and decay, the million-year old cycle of all life, takes place before our own eyes. Day by day. Everywhere. And we are part of the process too. We are full of admiration when we look at ancient trees, are fascinated by the elementary power of nature to always keep itself alive.
Alone the term national park creates a yearning for untouched nature in many of us. We find it directly at our doorstep. In the Kellerwald-Edersee National Park the forest goes its own way, haphazardly and always surprising. It shows decay and growth, often in the most confined spaces, reveals independence, unimaginable strength, diversity and beauty. When we dive into this forest, into the kingdom of quaint beeches, we are confronted with all of these facets wondering, maybe even startled or unsure.
But if we let it in, if we sharpen our senses, the fascinating wilderness will take hold of us.
This book wants to invite you to discover the redeveloping forest wilderness in the national park.
Enjoy an exciting expedition through the last native beech groves in Europe. The brilliant photographs and descriptions make this illustrated book an exclusive advertisement of a unique landscape in the north of Hessen.

# Inhalt / Contents

Impressum / Imprint .................................................................................................................................................. 2

Vorwort / Foreword .................................................................................................................................................. 3

Unser Naturerbe ist geschützt / Our natural heritage is protected ..................................................................... 6

Im Reich der urigen Buchen / In the kingdom of quaint beeches ..................................................................... 14

Faszination Wildnis / Fascinating wilderness ...................................................................................................... 46

Zeitfenster in die Erdgeschichte / Geological time-frame .................................................................................. 62

Klare Quellen und wilde Bäche / Clear springs and wild creeks ....................................................................... 72

Auf Spurensuche – sichtbare Geschichte / Looking for clues – visible history ................................................. 84

Edersee – ein „Fjord" im Kellerwald / Lake Eder – a „fjord" in the Kellerwald ................................................. 94

Bei Uhu, Wolf und Otter – ein Besuch im Wildpark / With eurasian eagle owl, wolf and otter – a visit to the wildlife park ................. 108

Wege in den Nationalpark / Routes into the national park ............................................................................. 118

Kurzinformationen / Short informations ........................................................................................................... 128

6 | UNSER NATURERBE IST GESCHÜTZT

OUR NATURAL HERITAGE IS PROTECTED | 7

Abendzauber im Nationalpark

*Enchantment of the night in the national park*

# Unser Naturerbe ist geschützt

*Natur Natur sein lassen – das mag an Wildnis im tropischen Regenwald mit Lianen und kreischenden Papageien erinnern. Doch echten Urwald, einen vom Menschen seit jeher nicht genutzten Wald, gibt es auch am Edersee.*

Um große Buchen-Urwälder zu erleben, muss man schon in die Slowakei, nach Rumänien oder in die Ukraine fahren. In Mitteleuropa sind nur winzige Reste der Axt entgangen, z. B. an wenigen abgelegenen Orten im Bayerischen Wald. Als sensationelle Entdeckung gelten die kleinflächigen Urwaldbereiche an unzugänglichen Steilhängen des nordhessischen Edersees, unter anderem in der Wooghölle am Nordhang des Arensberges.

Hessen ist Buchonia: Land der ausgedehnten Buchenwälder. Ein Schatz, dessen Wert vielen Menschen nicht bewusst ist, denn naturnahe Buchenwälder sind selten geworden. Deutschland gilt als Hauptverbreitungsgebiet und Hessen wiederum besitzt den höchsten Buchenanteil aller Bundesländer.

Mit der Ausweisung eines Buchen-Nationalparks im Kellerwald leistet Hessen einen unschätzbaren Beitrag zur Bewahrung unseres Naturerbes. Er hat den Rang einer Nationalen Naturlandschaft. Hier entwickelt sich unsere Wildnis von morgen.

Natur Natur sein lassen – das bedeutet die allmähliche Verwandlung eines früher forstlich genutzten Waldes in einen Naturwald, der vielleicht in einer Buchengeneration – also in etwa 300 Jahren – Urwaldcharakter haben wird. Ein Trost für alle Ungeduldigen: Der Weg dorthin ist spannend.

Für diesen Prozess sind die Kellerwaldberge südlich des Edersees hervorragend gerüstet: eines unserer größten geschlossenen Waldgebiete, ohne Siedlungen, nicht von Verkehrswegen durchschnitten und fast zur Gänze im Staatsbesitz. Wegen des schwierigen Geländes, aber auch weil einige Bereiche bereits lange Naturschutzgebiete waren, ist rund ein Viertel der Nationalparkfläche seit Jahrzehnten forstlich ungenutzt. Die Buche hat bereits heute einen Anteil von mehr als zwei Dritteln. Und ein besonderer Glücksfall: Jede dritte größere Buche ist älter als 120 Jahre und auf 1.000 ha finden wir Buchenwälder, die sogar älter als 160 Jahre sind.

Gemeinsam mit anderen deutschen Nationalparken – Jasmund auf Rügen, Hainich, Müritz (Serrahn), Bayerischer Wald und Eifel – steht der Nationalpark Kellerwald-Edersee für das europäische Naturerbe Buchenwald und ist zugleich mit seinen spezifischen, geologischen und klimatischen Bedingungen einzigartig. Schon heute erfüllt er weitgehend die Bedingungen der Internationalen Naturschutzunion (IUCN) für eine internationale Anerkennung. Kein Zweifel, der jüngste und zweitkleinste der 14 deutschen Nationalparke besitzt hervorragende Entwicklungschancen.

# Our natural heritage is protected

*Let nature be nature – this may call to mind the wilderness in a tropical rainforest with lianas and screaming parrots. But a true virgin forest, a forest not used by man since the beginning of time, can also be found on Lake Eder.*

To experience large beech groves, one has to travel as far as Slovakia, Romania or the Ukraine. Only minute remnants have been spared from the axe in Central Europe, e. g. in a few isolated places in the Bavarian Forest. The small patches of virgin forest on inaccessible steep slopes of Lake Eder in Northern Hessen, for example the Wooghölle on the north slope of the Arensberg, are regarded as a sensational discovery.

Hessen is Buchonia: Land of extensive beech forests, whose value many people are not aware of, because the natural beech forests have become rare. Germany constitutes the main geographic range and Hessen, in turn, possesses the highest share in beeches of all federal states.

Hessen's priceless contribution to the protection of our natural heritage is the acknowledgement of a beech national park in Kellerwald. It possesses the ranking of a national natural landscape. This is where our wilderness of tomorrow is developing.

Let nature be nature – that means the gradual change of a forest used previously for silviculture into a natural forest, which perhaps in one beech generation – in approximately 300 years, that is – will have the characteristics of a virgin forest. A consolation to those who are impatient: Getting there is enthralling.

The Kellerwald mountains in the south of Lake Eder are excellently prepared for such a process: one of our largest cohesive forest areas, without any settlements, free of intersecting roads and almost completely under public ownership. Due to the rough terrain, but also because some areas have been nature protection areas in the past, almost one fourth of the national park's surface has not been used for silviculture for decades. Already today, the share of beeches accounts for more than two thirds. And a particular piece of good fortune: of the larger beech trees, every third one is older than 120 years, and on 1,000 ha we find beech forest some of which are older than 160 years. Together with other German beech national parks – Jasmund on the island of Rügen, Hainich, Eifel, Müritz and Bayerischer Wald – the Kellerwald National Park represents the European natural heritage of the beech forest and at the same time is unique in terms of its specific geological and climatic conditions. Already today, it is able to fulfil the requirements of the International Union for Conservation of Nature and Natural Resources (IUCN) for international recognition. Without a doubt, the youngest and second smallest of the 14 German national parks possesses excellent potential for development.

O Täler weit,
o Höhen

*Oh valleys far,
oh mountains high*

OUR NATURAL HERITAGE IS PROTECTED | 11

Nationalpark
Kellerwald-Edersee
– Wald am Wasser

*Kellerwald-Edersee
National Park
– Forest at the water*

Durch ein Wald-
fenster in den
Nationalpark
geschaut

*View into the national
park through a window
of foliage*

OUR NATURAL HERITAGE IS PROTECTED | 13

Soweit das Auge schaut – ein Buchenmeer

*As far as the eye can see – a sea of beeches*

Buchen-Nationalpark
im Herzen
Deutschlands

*Beech national park in
the centre of Germany*

# Im Reich der urigen Buchen

*Natur Natur sein lassen – auf schmalem Pfad tauchen wir ein in das Buchenmeer, dort wo wir den Wald mit allen Sinnen erleben.*

Die Spitzen junger Buchen berühren sich über unseren Köpfen. Und dann die alten, urigen Bäume. Unser Blick wandert hinauf an den mächtigen Stämmen bis ins Kronendach. Wie alt mögen diese Baumriesen wohl sein? Sicher fast zweihundert Jahre. Ihr halbes Leben haben sie noch vor sich. Wir betasten die raue, rissige Rinde einer alten Buche am Wegrand. Dort ein prächtiger Bergahorn. Buchen-Nationalpark, weil die Rotbuche beherrschende Art ist, aber auch andere Baumarten finden hier ihren Platz: die Eichen am kargen, trockenen Südhang, Eschen und Ulmen in der feuchten Mulde, Linden im Blockschuttwald oder Erlen am Bergbach.

Faszinierend das Spiel von Licht und Schatten im Frühlingswald. Blitzende Strahlenbündel dringen durch das Blätterdach. Schattenspiel der Blätter auf silbern glänzender Rinde. Einfach die Augen schließen und den Stimmen des Waldes lauschen. Aus der Ferne tönt das lachende „krrü, krrü, krrü ..." eines Schwarzspechtes. Das ist die Erkennungsmelodie, wenn er durch sein Revier fliegt. Die vielen alten Buchen im Nationalpark Kellerwald sind für ihn ein Eldorado. Aber nicht nur für ihn, denn Schwarzspechte betreiben „sozialen Wohnungsbau". Alle paar Jahre zimmern sie neue Höhlen. Und die alten Behausungen finden zahlreiche Nachmieter: Raufußkauz, Hohltaube, Fledermäuse, Hornissen – bis hin zum Baummarder. Spechte sind im Nationalpark besonders bedeutsam, denn sie zeigen den Wandel des ehemals forstlich genutzten Waldes zur Wildnis an. Sechs Arten mit jeweils ganz spezifischen Lebensraumansprüchen haben die Vogelkundler erforscht.

Entlang des Berghangs streicht ein großer Greifvogel. Am gegabelten Schwanz erkennen wir den Roten Milan. Der elegante Flieger ist weltweit fast ausschließlich nur in Europa zu Hause – und der Kellerwald liegt mitten in seinem Verbreitungsgebiet. Auf dicken Buchen errichtet er seinen Horst. In den Wiesen und Feldern rings um den Nationalpark findet der Rote Milan ein reichhaltiges Nahrungsangebot. Auf alten Buchen brütet auch der Schwarzstorch. Ein bis zwei Paare ziehen alljährlich im Nationalpark ihre Jungen auf.

Da, ein Knacken im Unterholz. Ein Rothirsch überquert unseren Pfad. Welch eindrucksvolle Begegnung! Dass im Nationalpark größere Bestände dieser majestätischen Tiere erhalten geblieben sind, ist der Jagdgeschichte zu verdanken.

Die Dämmerung senkt sich über die Berge des Nationalparks. Der Waldkauz ruft. Eine erste Fledermaus umflattert an dem warmen Frühlingsabend die alten Buchen. Viele Geheimnisse birgt der Buchenwald – ein Erlebnis zu jeder Jahreszeit.

# In the kingdom of quaint beeches

*Let nature be nature – On narrow paths we dive into the sea of beeches where we experience the forest with all our senses.*

The tips of young beech trees touch above our heads. And look at the old, quaint trees! Our gaze wanders along the enormous trunks up to the tree top. How old might these tree giants be? Surely, almost 200 years old. They still have half their lives to live. We touch the rough, cracked bark of an old beech on the wayside. A grand sycamore is over there. Beech national park, because the Common beech is the dominant species, but also other tree species have found their place here: the oaks on the meagre, dry southern slope, ash trees and elm trees in the humid vale, lime trees in the ravine forest or alders in the mountain creek.

Fascinating is the play of light and shadow in the forest in spring. Twinkling bundles of rays penetrate the roof of leaves. Shadows of leaves play on the silver shining bark. Just close your eyes and listen to the sounds of the forest. The laughing „krru, krru, krru ..." of a black woodpecker sounds from far away. This is the signature tune when it flies through its territory. The many old beeches in the Kellerwald National Park are the black woodpecker's paradise, but not exclusively, since black woodpeckers practise „social housing". Every other year they build new caves and the old housing finds numerous new tenants: boreal owl, stock dove, bats, hornets – and also the sweet marten. Woodpeckers are of special importance in the national park since they signify the transition of the forest used previously for silviculture to wilderness. Ornithologists have researched six species, each of which has very unique habitat requirements.

A large bird of prey sweeps along the mountain side. The forked tail tells us that it is a red kite. The home of this elegant flyer is almost exclusively in Europe – and the Kellerwald is in the centre of where it prevails. It builds its eyrie on massive beeches. In the meadows and fields surrounding the national park, red kites find a rich food supply. The black stork breeds on old beeches. Every year, one or two couples raise their young in the national park.

Listen, cracking in the underwood. A red deer crosses our path. What an impressive encounter! Thanks to the tradition of hunting in the past, large populations of these majestic animals could be preserved in the national park.

Night falls on the national park's mountains. The tawny owl calls. The first bat flutters around the old beeches on the warm spring evening. The beech forest holds many secrets – an adventure at any time of the year.

Lichtspiele im
Buchenwald

*Reflections of light in
the beech forest*

Herbstgold

*Autumn gold*

Sonnenstrahlen durchdringen den Nebel.

*Rays of sun shine through the fog.*

**Schwarzspecht und seine Nachmieter:** Hohltaube unten links und Raufußkauz unten rechts

*Black woodpecker and its next tenants:* stock dove bottom left and boreal owl bottom right

IN THE KINGDOM OF QUAINT BEECHES | 21

Der Kleinspecht benötigt zum Zimmern seiner Bruthöhle morsche Baumstämme.

*The lesser spotted woodpecker needs rotten tree trunks to build its brooding cave.*

Der Mittelspecht ist nach dem Buntspecht die häufigste Spechtart im Nationalpark.

*The middle spotted woodpecker is the most common woodpecker species in the national park following the great spotted woodpecker.*

Der Grauspecht gilt als Leitart der Bergbuchenwälder.

*The grey-headed woodpecker is considered the leading species of the mountain beech forests.*

Das erste Grün
im Ruhlauber

*The first green sprout
in Ruhlauber*

Nur für kurze Zeit
zeigt sich im Mai das
Buchenlaub so zart
und frisch.

*Only in May and for a
very short time do the
beech leaves show such
fragility and freshness.*

Morgendliche Sonnenstrahlen vergolden das Frühlingslaub.

*Morning rays of sun gilding spring leaves.*

Am Arensberg: sattes Grün zur Sommerzeit

*At Arensberg: rich green in the summer time*

Herbstimpressionen

*Autumnal impressions*

Winterstimmungen

Winter moods

**Jäger auf lautlosen Schwingen:**
der Uhu

*Hunter on soundless wings:*
*The eurasian eagle owl*

Was ist da los?

*What's going on here?*

**Imposante Buchen**
*Impressive beeches*

Mächtige Buche am Ruhlauber

*Giant beech at Ruhlauber*

Uralte Hutebuche bei Bringhausen – dickste Buche im Nationalpark?

*Ancient pedunculate beech near Bringhausen – thickest beech in the national park?*

Vor Jahrzehnten verletzt: Die Zeit heilt auch große Wunden.

*Injured decades ago: Time also heals large wounds.*

Im Hochzeitskleid: Kaisermantel an Brombeerblüte

*Wearing a wedding dress: silver-washed fritillary on a blackberry blossom*

Die Larven des Buchenbocks entwickeln sich unter der Rinde und im Holz von Rotbuchen.

*The larvae of the capricorn beetle develop under the bark and in the wood of red beeches.*

Die Raupe des Buchen-Rotschwanzes lebt von Sommer bis Herbst auf verschiedenen Laubbäumen.

*The caterpillar of the pale tussock moth lives on various deciduous trees from summer until autumn.*

Erdkröten-Pärchen auf dem Weg zum Laichgewässer

*Common toad couple on their way to the spawning ground*

Am liebsten mag die scheue Gelbhalsmaus Buchen- und Eichen-Hainbuchenwälder mit Haselnussbüschen.

*The shy yellow-necked mouse prefers beech and oak-hornbeam-forests with hazelnut trees.*

**Großwild im Kellerwald**
*Big game in the Kellerwald*

Rivalenkampf im September

*Fight between rivals in September*

Der Herbst hat den Tisch reich mit Bucheckern gedeckt.

*Autumn brought an abundance of beech-nuts.*

Wo Hase und Fuchs sich Gute Nacht sagen …

*In the middle of nowhere …*

Die seltene Elsbeere ist mit der Eberesche verwandt.

*The rare wild service-tree is related to the mountain ash.*

Spitz-Ahorn: Blütenrispe

*Norway maple: the flower panicle*

Ahornbäume am Daudenberg im Blütenschmuck

*Maple trees in blossom on Daudenberg*

Die Mehlbeere entfaltet ihre Blätter.

*The common whitebeam unfolds its leaves.*

Markante Strukturen eines alten Hainbuchenstammes

*Prominent structures of an old hornbeam trunk*

Frühlingsblüher im Schutz einer Buche: Buschwindröschen

*Spring flowers under the protection of a beech: anemones*

Weiße Hainsimse – Charakterart der Buchenwälder im Nationalpark

*White wood-rush – Characteristic species of the national park's beech forests*

Bild rechts: Rot leuchten die reifen Beeren des Aronstabs im August.

*Picture on the right: The ripe berries of the lords-and-ladies shine in August.*

Schon im Vorfrühling lockt der Seidelbast mit intensivem Duft die ersten Insekten.

*Already in early spring, the intense fragrance of daphne attracts the first insects.*

Das Schwertblättrige Waldvöglein ist eine Orchidee.

*The sword-leaved helleborine is an orchid.*

## Bemerkenswerte Pilze
### Impressive fungi

Ästiger Stachelbart – ein Naturwaldzeiger

*Bear's head tooth – an indication of a natural forest*

Buchenschleimrübling – Charakterart alter Buchenwälder

*Porcelain mushroom – Characteristic species of old beech forests*

Buchen-Keimling

*Beech seedling*

Selten zusammen: junges Grün und alter Fruchtbecher einer Buche

*Rarely seen together: Fresh green and old cupule of a beech*

Das Große Mausohr hat eine Wochenstube in der Vöhler Kirche, sein nächtliches Jagdrevier im Nationalpark.

*The greater mouse-eared bat resides in the Vöhler church by day and hunts in the national park by night.*

Der Schwarzstorch brütet im Nationalpark und jagt auch in stillen Tälern außerhalb.

*The black stork breeds in the national park and also goes hunting in the quiet valleys beyond.*

Der Kolkrabe: Jahrzehntelang ausgestorben, zieht der bussardgroße Vogel wieder seine Kreise über dem Kellerwald.

*The raven: extinct for decades, the buzzard-sized bird circles over the Kellerwald once again.*

Der majestätische Rotmilan – größter heimischer Greifvogel – hat das Zentrum seines weltweiten Verbreitungsgebietes in Nordhessen und Thüringen.

*The worldwide distribution of the majestic red kite – the largest domestic bird of prey – is centred in northern Hessen and Thuringia.*

**Licht und Schatten**
Werden und Vergehen

*Light and shadow*
*Growth and decay*

Neues Grün auf morschen Ästen

*New green on rotten branches*

# Faszination Wildnis

*Natur Natur sein lassen – das bedeutet Wildnis wagen. Wälder ohne Nutzung und Gestaltung sind Orte der Wildnis von morgen. Sie können Menschen begeistern, Sehnsüchte stillen. Denn Wildnis beinhaltet Faszinierendes und Geheimnisvolles, ist Inbegriff für Freiheit und Abenteuer.*

Eine Reaktion auf die fortschreitende Naturzerstörung unserer Tage ist die Wiederentdeckung der Wildnis. Groß ist die Zahl der Angebote zu diesem Thema: Wildnistouren und Erleben von Wildnis in fernen Ländern, aber auch Wildnis entdecken vor der eigenen Haustür.

Im Kellerwald wird eine von Menschenhand geprägte Landschaft der Natur zurückgegeben. Wildnis von morgen? Auf kleiner Fläche können wir ihr schon heute im Nationalpark begegnen. In der Wooghölle, einem Steilhang des Arensbergs am Edersee, hat wahrscheinlich ein echter Urwald die Zeiten überdauert. Soweit die Forstchronik zurückreicht, bis ins frühe 19. Jahrhundert, erklang hier keine Axt. Weit über 200 Jahre alte Buchen und Linden beherrschen das Bild. Wir erreichen die Wooghölle über den Urwaldsteig, einen der schönsten deutschen Wanderwege. Rund um den Edersee über Stock und Stein führt er auf verschlungenen Pfaden. Der Urwaldsteig bietet unvergessliche Ausblicke auf Edersee und Nationalpark und eröffnet die Möglichkeit, am Nordufer des Edersees weitere Urwaldreste oder Naturwälder naturverträglich zu entdecken. Lindenberg, Kahle Hardt, Mühlecke und Kanzel bieten authentische Eindrücke von Wildnis.

Eindrucksvolle alte Baumgestalten im Nationalpark sind Symbol für Wildnis. Mit den Jahren – so sagt Alexander Demandt in seiner Kulturgeschichte des Baumes – gewinnen Bäume an Charakter, Individualität und verkörpern „sichtbar gewachsene Geschichte". Alte, knorrige Bäume stehen für freie Entfaltung der Natur. Ihre bizarren Gestalten beflügeln besonders bei Nebel unsere Phantasie und führen uns in die Welt der Kobolde und Gnome.

Und spannend ist es schließlich auch, die Entwicklung des alten Kulturwaldes hin zur neuen Wildnis zu erleben. Wandern wir zum Ruhlauber, einem herrlichen alten Buchenwald nördlich der Quernstkirche. Bereits 1989 wurde er zum Naturschutzgebiet erklärt. Damals ohne Unterwuchs – heute ein schönes Beispiel für einen naturnahen Wald. Hier und da ist bereits eine zweihundertjährige Buche umgefallen und macht Platz für die nächste Baumgeneration. Pilze und ein grünes Moosskleid zeigen an, dass der vermodernde Stamm vielen Tieren einen Lebensraum bietet, z. B. zahlreichen Käferarten, die auf totes Holz spezialisiert sind und nur hier existieren können. Ganz allmählich holt die Natur den gefallenen Riesen zurück in ihren Schoß.

Wildnis zulassen, heißt unser Naturerbe bewahren. Denn unbeeinflusst vom Menschen entfaltet der Wald eine eigene Dynamik. Der Baum stirbt eines natürlichen Todes, reißt eine Lücke in den Wald, vermodert und ermöglicht neues Leben. Zu Lebzeiten hat er vorgesorgt. Seine Samen sind gekeimt. Junge Bäume haben nur auf Licht gewartet, um die Kronenherrschaft zu übernehmen. Es ist ein ewiger Zyklus von Werden und Vergehen. Jedes Tier und jede Pflanze kämpft ständig um Raum – ein Kampf, der die natürliche Artenvielfalt im Wald ausmacht. Nur Naturgewalten wie Eis, Sturm und Blitz unterbrechen den Zyklus, spiegeln sich in gefallenen und gespaltenen Stämmen. Bis auch hier ein Neuanfang das Sterben einholt und die Lücken im Wald wieder geschlossen werden.

Wildnis im Nationalpark – das sind auch die ursprünglichen Felsgruppen, Blockhalden, Quellen, Bäche und viele andere Schöpfungen der Natur.

# Fascinating wilderness

*Let nature be nature – that means give nature a chance. Forest without utilisation and design are places of tomorrow's wilderness. They can inspire people, satisfy desires. Because wilderness contains something fascinating and mysterious, is the epitome of freedom and adventure.*

One response to the progressive destruction of nature in our time is the rediscovery of wilderness. The number of offers on this topic is enormous: wilderness tours and wilderness experience in remote countries, but also discovering wilderness at one's own doorstep.

In the Kellerwald, a landscape marked by man is being returned to its natural state. The wilderness of tomorrow? Even today, it's visible in small areas of the national park. In the Wooghölle, a steep slope of the Arensberg on Lake Eder, a true virgin forest has survived time. As far back as the history of the forest can be traced, into the 19th century, no axe could be heard. More than 200-year old beeches and lime trees dominate the forest's image. We arrive at the Wooghölle via the Urwaldsteig, one of Germany's most beautiful hiking trails. It follows the perimeter of Lake Eder over rough and smooth labrynthine paths. The Urwaldsteig offers unforgettable views over Lake Eder and the national park, and offers the possibility to discover other remnants of virgin and natural forests on the northern shore in a nature-friendly way. Lindenberg, Kahle Hardt, Mühlecke and Kanzel offer authentic impressions of wilderness.

Impressive old tree shapes in the national park are a symbol of wilderness. Over the years – as Alexander Demandt tells in his cultural history of the tree – trees gain in character, individuality and embody „visibly grown history". Old, gnarly trees stand for the free development of nature. Their bizarre shapes fire our imagination, especially in the mist, and lead us into the world of goblins and gnomes.

And, it is also exciting after all to experience the development of the old cultural forest into a new wilderness. Let's hike to the Ruhlauber, an old beautiful beech grove to the north of the Quernstkirche (church). It was already declared a nature protection area in 1989. At that time, it had no scrub – today a good example of a forest close to nature. Here and there a 200-year old beech has already toppled down and made way for the next generation of trees. Fungi and a cover of green moss indicate that the rotten trunk offers a habitat for many creatures, e. g. numerous beetle species that specialise in dead wood and can only exist there. Gradually, nature returns the fallen giant to its fold.

Accepting wilderness means to protect our natural heritage, because the forest develops its own dynamic when no influence is exercised. The tree dies a natural death, leaves a gap in the forest and facilitates the development of new life. In its lifetime it has made provisions. Its seeds have sprouted. Young trees have only waited for the light to assume the reign of the tree tops. It's an eternal cycle of growth and decay. Every animal and every plant is constantly fighting for space – a fight which accounts for the natural diversity of species in the forest. Only natural forces of nature such as ice, storm and lightning disrupt the cycle, reflected in the fallen and split trunks. Until a new beginning catches up with death and closes the gaps in the forest.
Wilderness in the national park – that also includes the original rock formations, boulder fields, springs, creeks and many other creations of nature.

Wooghölle am Arensberg

*Wooghölle at Arensberg*

Im unwegsamen Blockhaldenwald – erstaunlich, dass auf solchen Felsbrocken Linden wachsen können.

*In the impassable boulder field forest – astonishing that lime trees can grow on such boulders.*

Bizarrer Buchenveteran an der Wooghölle – eindrucksvoll zu jeder Jahreszeit

*Bizarre beech veteran at the Wooghölle – impressive in all seasons*

Am Traddelkopf: auf dem Weg zur Wildnis

*At Traddelkopf: on the way into the wilderness*

Im Ruhlauber: Der Wald wird vielschichtig.

*At Ruhlauber: The forest becomes manifold.*

Totes Holz bleibt im natürlichen Zyklus.

*Dead wood remains in the cycle of nature.*

Alte Eiche zwischen Hemfurth und Bringhausen

*Old oak between Hemfurth and Bringhausen*

Markante Baumruine
– ein lebendiger Ort

*Distrinctive tree ruin
– a lively place*

Der Eulenbaum

*The owl tree*

„Kirchenfenster"
im Buchenwald

*„Church window"
in the beech grove*

Wildnis am einsamen
Waldbach

*Wilderness on a lonely
forest creek*

Die hohle Buche bietet Schutz.

*The hollow beech offers shelter.*

Naturerbe am nördlichen Ederseehang: 1.000 Jahre alte Eichen an der „Kahlen Hardt"

*Natural heritage on Lake Eder: 1,000 year-old oak at the „Kahlen Hardt"*

Abenteuer Wildnis – urige Bäume entdecken am Urwaldsteig

*Experience wilderness – discover old trees along the Urwaldsteig*

Kobolde, Gnome und „Schlangenbäume" am Hagenstein

*Goblins, gnomes and „snake trees" on the Hagenstein*

Bald wird der morsche Stamm im Kreislauf der Natur vergehen.

*Soon the rotten trunk will decay in the cycle of nature.*

Der Wanderweg rund um den Daudenberg vermittelt den besten Eindruck von einer Blockhalde.

*The hiking trail leading around the Daudenberg conveys the best impression of a boulder field.*

# Zeitfenster in die Erdgeschichte

*Natur Natur sein lassen – das können wir gelassen sehen, wenn wir die gewaltigen Zeiträume der Erdgeschichte bedenken. Vor 300 bis 400 Millionen Jahren war der heutige Kellerwald von einem Meer bedeckt.*

Als östlicher Ausläufer des Rheinischen Schiefergebirges entstand der Kellerwald durch Auffaltung sehr alter Meeresablagerungen. Tonschiefer und Grauwacke sind seine beiden Hauptgesteinsarten.

Durch die langsame Anhebung des Mittelgebirges haben sich die Gewässer tief in weichere Partien des Gesteins eingeschnitten. So ist z. B. der steil aufragende Hagenstein, im Volksmund Edertaler Loreley genannt, ein ehemaliger Prallhang der Eder. Die härteren Gesteine sind stehen geblieben und bilden die Bergrücken. Auf diese Weise entstand die charakteristische Landschaft mit ihrem ständigen Wechsel von Bergen und Tälern.

Im Bereich der Quernst bei Altenlotheim entdecken wir ein Gestein, das auf den ersten Blick wie grober Beton aussieht. Zahlreiche kleine Kieselsteine sind hier in eine kieselig-tonige Masse eingebettet. Dieses sogenannte Konglomeratgestein ist ebenso wie der Tonschiefer und die Grauwacke eine Meeresablagerung. Schöne Exemplare kann man entlang des Weges zwischen Quernst und Ruhlauber betrachten.

Das Faszinierendste, was der Nationalpark Hobbygeologen zu bieten hat, sind die zahlreichen Blockhalden. Diese eröffnen Zeitfenster in die waldfreie Nacheiszeit. Im Laufe der letzten 10.000 Jahre vermochte kein Wald diese extremen Standorte zu erobern. Die Entstehung einer solchen Halde kann man gut am Westhang des Daudenberges studieren. Im Laufe der Jahrtausende drang immer wieder Wasser in die Spalten der Grauwacke ein, Frost und Hitze sprengten die Felsen und bildeten so die Geröllhalde.

Über Jahrtausende nahezu unverändert geblieben sind auch die Felsen mit dem botanischen Juwel des Nationalparks, der Pfingstnelke. Seit der nacheiszeitlichen Wärmeperiode konnte sich diese Pflanze z. B. am Bloßenberg bei Bringhausen behaupten. Wir staunen darüber, wie die Urahnin unserer Gartennelke es schafft, mit den extremen Lebensbedingungen fertig zu werden. Die steilen Tonschieferwände bieten ihr kaum Schutz vor Sonne und Frost; Wasser und Nährstoffe sind Mangelware. Im Sommer steigen die Temperaturen auf bis zu 60 Grad Celsius, im Winter sind es bisweilen unter minus 20 Grad Celsius. Ein polsterförmiger Wuchs und nadelförmige, mit Wachs überzogene Blätter schützen die Überlebenskünstlerin vor dem Vertrocknen. Ihre Wurzeln dringen tief in die Felsspalten ein.

Fenster, die geologische Einblicke gewähren, sind auch die ehemaligen Steinbrüche und Bergwerksstollen. Die längste Geschichte hat wohl der Bleiberg oberhalb des Banfetals. Seit Mitte des 16. Jahrhunderts schürften hier Bergleute nach silberhaltigem Bleierz. Im 18. Jahrhundert entdeckten sie am Fuße des Berges auch Kupfererz. In diesem Stollen überwintern heute Fledermäuse. Die Goldlöcher am Rabenstein bei Affoldern erinnern an Zeiten, als man dort vergeblich nach dem edlen Metall suchte.

# Geological time-frame

*Let nature be nature – we can simply wait and see considering the vast periods of the earth's history. Between 300 and 400 million years ago, today's Kellerwald was covered by an ocean.*

As the eastern foothills of the Rhenish Slate Mountains, the Kellerwald developed through the upfolding of extremely old oceanic sediments. Clay slate and greywacke are its two major rock types.

Due to the slow elevation of the low mountain ranges, the waters cut deep into the softer parts of the rock. The steep towering Hagenstein, for example, legendary as the Loreley of the Eder Valley, used to be an undercut slope of the River Eder. The harder rocks remained, and now form the mountain ridge. This is how the typical landscape developed with its continuous alternation of mountains and valleys.

In the area of the Quernst (mountain) near Altenlotheim, we discover a rock which on first sight appears to be rough concrete. Many small pebbles are embedded in a mass of pebbles and clay. This so called conglomerate rock is also oceanic sediment as are clay slate and greywacke. Good examples can be observed along the trail between Quernst and Ruhlauber.

The most fascinating the national park has to offer to hobby geologists are the numerous boulder fields. These open up time-frames into the forest-free ice and post ice age. Over the course of the past 10,000 years, no forest was able to conquer this extreme location.

The development of such a field may be studied perfectly on the western slope of the Daudenberg. Over the course of thousands of years, water repeatedly penetrated the cracks of greywacke and frost, and heat burst the rocks and formed boulder fields.

The rocks on which the botanical jewel of the national park, the fire witch, grows have also remained almost unchanged over thousands of years. Ever since the warm period following the post ice age, this plant has been able to sustain itself, for example on Bloßenberg near Bringhausen. We marvel at how the ancestor of our common carnation is able to cope with such extreme environmental conditions. The steep clay slate walls offer scarce protection from the sun and frost, and water and nutrients are in short supply. Temperatures rise up to 60 °C in the summer and sometimes fall below minus 20 °C in winter. A cushion-like growth and needle-shaped leaves covered in wax protect the skilled survivor from withering. Its roots reach deep into the crevices.

Former quarries and pits are also time-frames offering geological insights. The Bleiberg situated above the Banfetal has probably the longest history. From the middle of the 16th century, miners dug here for silver-containing galena. In the 18th century they also discovered copper ore at the bottom of the mountain. Today these mines are the hibernation quarter for bats in winter. The gold pits at Rabenstein near Affoldern recall times when people tried in vain to dig up the precious metal.

Bizarre Grauwacke-Felsen im Buchenmeer

*Bizarre greywacke rock in a sea of beeches*

Blockhalde: Rings von Wald umgeben, aber seit der Eiszeit hatten Bäume hier keine Chance.

*Boulder field: Surrounded by woods, but since the ice age trees didn't stand a chance here.*

Tonschiefer enthält bisweilen auch andere Mineralien, die ihn bunt färben.

*Clay slate sometimes also contains other minerals which lend it colour.*

Eine Baumwurzel bringt den Tonschiefer an den Tag.

*A tree root reveals clay slate.*

Das Konglomeratgestein an der Hummelwiese ist aus einer Meeresablagerung entstanden.

*The conglomerate rocks along the Hummelwiese developed from oceanic sediment.*

Überwiegend besteht es aus Kieselsteinen, die in ein kieselig-toniges Bindemittel eingelagert sind.

*It consists primarily of pebbles which are embedded in a bond of pebbles and clay.*

Bunte Welt der Flechten – formenreiche Doppelwesen aus Pilzen und Algen

*Colourful world of lichen – double-natured proliferation of forms – fungi and algae*

Versteckt in Felsspalten wurzelt der Braunstielige Streifenfarn.

*Hidden in crevices, the maidenhair spleenwort fern takes root.*

Die seltene Schlingnatter ist die einzige Schlangenart im Nationalpark. Das ungiftige Tier sonnt sich gern auf Felsen.

*The rare smooth snake is the only snake species in the Kellerwald. The non-poisonous reptile likes to sunbathe on rocks.*

Bild rechts: Zwei Überlebenskünstler in der Felswand: Pfingstnelke und Tüpfelfarn

*Picture on the right: Two skilled survivors on a rock face: fire witch and rock cap fern*

Erlen-Galerie im Kessbachtal

*Gallery of alders in the Kessbachtal*

# Klare Quellen und wilde Bäche

*Natur Natur sein lassen – mehr als 500 Quellen entspringen aus den Tiefen der Kellerwaldberge. Ihr klares Wasser bietet seltenen Tierarten einen einzigartigen Lebensraum.*

Unberührte Quellen sind selten geworden in unserer Kulturlandschaft. In den natürlichen Quellen des Nationalparks fühlen sich selbst Lebewesen wohl, die allerhöchste Ansprüche an die Güte des Wassers stellen – wie etwa der Alpenstrudelwurm oder die Quellschnecke. So ist der Alpenstrudelwurm eigentlich ein Bewohner eiskalter Gebirgsbäche. In den Quellen des Kellerwaldes konnte er seit der letzten Eiszeit überleben. Der lichtscheue kleine Wurm versteckt sich auf der Unterseite von Laub und Steinen, als Nahrung dienen ihm winzige Krebse. Versiegt die Quelle im heißen Sommer, zieht er sich ins dunkle Grundwasser zurück. Die winzige Quellschnecke ist kleiner als ein Streichholzkopf. Ebenso wie der Alpenstrudelwurm hat die in Deutschland bedrohte Art die Jahrtausende seit der Eiszeit überdauert. Schon auf geringe Temperaturschwankungen ihres kühlen Lebensraumes reagiert sie sehr empfindlich. Aus ihrem Dasein schließen die Forscher, dass die Kellerwaldberge schon seit sehr langen Zeiten bewaldet sind.

Die Quellrinnsale des Nationalparks vereinigen sich zu sprudelnden Waldbächen, deren Wasserqualität ebenfalls ausgezeichnet ist. Weitgehend unbeeinflusst von Menschenhand schlängeln sie sich durch die Täler, gesäumt von altehrwürdigen Erlen. Seichte Bereiche wechseln mit tiefen, steile Ufer mit flachen, und an vielen Stellen entstehen Sandbänke und Strudellöcher. Alles, was einen lebendigen Bach ausmacht. Hundsbach, Bärenbach, Kessbach, Banfe und Mellbach münden in den Edersee.

In den Bergbächen tummeln sich Köcherfliegen-Larven, Bachforelle oder auch die Groppe, eine europaweit geschützte Fischart. Für die anspruchsvolle Larve des Feuersalamanders sind sie eine ideale Kinderstube. Zahlreiche Elterntiere – auffällig schwarzgelb gefärbt – leben daher in den ausgedehnten Buchenwäldern. Am Arensberg, im Kessbach- oder Hundsbachtal sind sie zu hunderten zu finden. Und auch die charakteristischen Vögel natürlicher Bergbäche – Wasseramsel, Eisvogel und Gebirgsstelze – kann der aufmerksame Wanderer im Nationalpark entdecken.

# Clear springs and wild creeks

*Let nature be nature – more than 500 springs originate from the depths of the Kellerwald mountains. Their clear water offers a unique habitat for rare animal species.*

Pristine springs have become rare in our cultural landscape. Even species requiring the highest quality of water – such as the flatworm Crenobia alpine and Bythinella dunkeri – feel comfortable in the natural springs of the national park. Crenobia alpine actually lives in ice-cold mountaine creeks. It was able to survive the last ice age in the Kellerwald springs. The small photophobic worm hides underneath leaves and stones; it eats minute crustaceans. When the spring dries in summer, it retreats into the dark ground water. The minute Bythinella dunkeri is smaller than a match head. Like Crenobia alpine, this species, which is endangered in Germany, has survived the millenniums since the ice age. It responds very sensitively to even slight fluctuations in the temperature of its cool habitat. Researchers have concluded from its existence that the Kellerwald mountains have been wooded for ages.

The spring runlets unite to form sputtering forest creeks whose water quality is also excellent. To a large extent unaffected by man's influence, they meander through the valleys lined with time-honoured alders. Shallow parts alternate with deep, steep banks with flat, and in many places sandbanks and potholes have developed. Everything that characterises a living creek. Hundsbach, Bärenbach, Kessbach, Banfe and Mellbach flow into Lake Eder.

Caddisfly larvae, brown trout and also the bullhead, a fish species protected throughout Europe, cavort in the mountain creeks. They are an ideal nursery for the demanding larvae of the fire salamander. Therefore numerous parents – in conspicuous black and yellow markings – live in the extensive beech forests. Hundreds of them can be found at Arensberg, in the Kessbachtal or Hundsbachtal. And also the characteristic birds of natural mountain creeks – dipper, kingfisher and grey wagtail – can be discovered by the attentive hiker.

Elsebachquelle
bei Schmittlotheim

*Elsebach spring
near Schmittlotheim*

Milzkraut
– Charakterpflanze
der Quellbereiche

*Golden saxifrage
– characteristic plant
of spring areas*

Man muss schon
genau hinschauen,
um die unscheinbare
Sickerquelle zu
entdecken.

*One has to take a
really close look to
discover the
inconspicuous marsh.*

Sickerquelle unterhalb einer sechsstämmigen Buche zwischen Fahrentriesch und Schmittlotheim

*Marsh below a six-trunk beech between Fahrentriesch and Schmittlotheim*

Wie ein kleiner Drache aus Urzeiten mutet die Groppe an.

*The bullhead looks like a small dragon from primitive times.*

Unter den heimischen Amphibien haben Feuersalamander die engste Bindung an den Wald. An warmen Tagen begegnen uns die nachtaktiven Tiere nach starkem Regen.

*Among the domestic amphibians, fire salamanders have the strongest tie to the forest. On warm days after heavy rainfalls we can encounter these nocturnal animals.*

Dreiklang von Bach, Wald und Wiese

*Triad of creek, forest and meadow*

Auch kleine Wasserfälle machen großen Eindruck.

*Small waterfalls are also impressive.*

Naturnaher Buchenwald und lebendiger Bergbach

*Beech forest close to nature and lively mountain creek*

Oberhalb des ehemaligen Fischteichs im unteren Banfetal hat sich ein prächtiger Erlen-Bruchwald entwickelt.

*A magnificent swampy alder wood has developed above the former fish pond in the lower Banfetal.*

Bild rechts: Typisch für manche Quellen im Nationalpark ist die Ablagerung von rot-gelbem Eisenocker.

*Picture on the right: The red-yellow sediment of iron oxide is typical of some springs in the national park.*

Der farbenprächtige Eisvogel ist regelmäßiger Gast am Banfeteich. Dort erbeutet er kleine Fischchen.

*The colourful kingfisher is a regular guest of the Banfeteich (pond). Here, it captures small fish.*

Die Wasseramsel taucht selbst im eiskalten Bergbach nach Insekten. Sie brütet an Kessbach und Banfe.

*The dipper enjoys diving after insects even in the ice-cold mountain creek. It breeds on the Kessbach and Banfe.*

Schillerndes Juwel am Bergbach: die Gebänderte Prachtlibelle

*Dazzling jewel at the mountain creek: the banded demoiselle*

Aus winzigen Kieselsteinchen haben Köcherfliegenlarven ihre Behausungen gebaut.

*Caddisflies larvae have built their abode from minute pebbles.*

Das Fahrentriesch
– eine alte
Rodungsinsel des
Zisterzienserklosters
Haina

*The Fahrentriesch
– an old isolated
clearing of the Haina
Cistercian monastery*

# Auf Spurensuche – sichtbare Geschichte

*Natur Natur sein lassen – ist heute das Motto des Nationalparks. Aber über viele Jahrhunderte hinweg nutzten die Menschen den Kellerwald und prägten so das Landschaftsbild des heutigen Nationalparks. Begeben wir uns auf Spurensuche.*

Mitten im Wald finden sich Hügelgräber aus der Bronzezeit. Sie sind die frühesten menschlichen Zeugnisse, die wir im Nationalpark entdecken können. Etwa 800 bis 1.000 Jahre vor Christi wurden sie als Einzelgräber angelegt.

Rodungsinseln im Westen des Nationalparks geben uns Hinweise auf ehemalige Bewohner des Waldes. Im 13. und 14. Jahrhundert gründete hier das nahegelegene Zisterzienserkloster Haina kleine Siedlungen, die von den Waldbauern jedoch bald wieder aufgegeben wurden. Zu unwirtlich war das Klima, zu karg der Boden. Vielleicht raffte auch die Pest die Siedler dahin. Wir wissen es nicht.

Auf den Wiesen und Feldern der verlassenen Siedlungen ließen Bauern aus den benachbarten Dörfern Rinder und Schafe grasen. So entstanden die „Triescher" – brachgefallenes Land, das als Gemeinschaftsweide genutzt wurde. An einer besonderen Grasart, dem Borstgras, können Botaniker noch heute erkennen, dass die Flächen einst beweidet wurden. Am besten erhalten ist das Fahrentriesch in der Nähe des Ortes Altenlotheim.

Bis ins 19. Jahrhundert trieben die Menschen ihr Vieh in den Kellerwald. Daran erinnern auch die uralten Triftwege, z. B. bei Kleinern, Asel und Altenlotheim. Noch heute stehen im Nationalpark knorrige, alte Hutebuchen und -eichen, deren Früchte einst für die Schweine willkommenes Futter boten. Unsere Spurensuche führt uns außerdem zu alten Hohlwegen, auf denen sich die Räder der Ochsenkarren über Jahrhunderte hinweg bei der Holzabfuhr in den Waldboden eingegraben haben.

In den Buchenwäldern des Nationalparks stoßen wir allenthalben auf flache, runde Plätze von etwa zehn Metern Durchmesser. Wer an einer solchen Stelle mit dem Fuß das Laub beiseite schiebt, kann eine schwarze Bodenschicht erkennen. Vor 150 oder 200 Jahren rauchte hier einmal ein Kohlenmeiler. Schätzungsweise fünfhundert solcher Köhlerplatten verteilen sich über den gesamten Nationalpark.

Ein kulturhistorisch bedeutender Platz ist die ehemalige Quernstkirche zwischen Altenlotheim und Frebershausen. Nur noch flache, von Gras überwachsene Wälle lassen den Grundriss des 1230 erstmals urkundlich erwähnten Gotteshauses erahnen. Nach der Reformation verfiel es mehr und mehr und seine Steine wurden zum Hausbau in Altenlotheim verwendet. So abgelegen, wie es heute scheinen will, war die Kirche damals nicht. Auf ihrem Friedhof begruben die Bewohner der benachbarten Dörfer ihre Toten. Am 3. Mai eines jeden Jahres, dem Kreuztag, fand dort ein großer Jahrmarkt statt. Die Stadt Frankenau errichtete 2006 an diesem historischen Ort eine Kapelle: ein Ort der Andacht und der Ehrfurcht, eine Möglichkeit zum stillen Dialog mit der Natur.

Dass die herrlichen Wiesentäler im Nationalpark erhalten blieben, verdanken wir der Jagdleidenschaft früherer Generationen: Schon Hainaer Äbte und Waldecker Fürsten erlegten in diesen Gebieten kapitale Hirsche.

# Looking for clues – visible history

*Let nature be nature – is today the slogan of national park. But the Kellerwald has been used by people over many centuries, thus shaping the landscape of today's national park. Lets go looking for clues.*

In the midst of the forest are burial mounds from the Bronze Age. These are the earliest traces of human evidence we can discover in the national park. Between approximately 800 and 1,000 years B. C., these were laid out as individual graves.

Isolated clearings in the west of the national park hint at former inhabitants of the forest. In the 13th and 14th centuries, the nearby Haina Cistercian monastery founded small settlements here, which were soon afterwards abandoned by the farmers, however. The climate was just too rough and the soil too meagre. Maybe the settlers were decimated by the plague. We don't know.

Farmers of the neighbouring villages let their cattle and sheep graze in the meadows of the abandoned settlement. This is how „Triescher" developed – fallow land which was used as common pasture land. Based on a particular type of grass, the matgrass, botanists can still perceive today that the area was once used as pasture land. The Fahrentriesch near Altenlotheim is the best preserved.
The people drove their cattle into the Kellerwald until the 19th century. The ancient trails, e. g. near Kleinern, Asel and Altenlotheim also remind us of this. Even today, gnarly pedunculate beeches and oaks, the fruits of which were once welcomed as feed for pigs, still stand in the national park. In the search for clues, we also come across old narrow paths on which the wheels of oxen carts transporting wood dug deep into the forest floor over the centuries.

All about the beech forests of the national park we come across flat, round areas with diameters of approximately 10 meters. If you push the leaves aside with your foot, you will discover a black layer on the ground. A charcoal stack once smouldered here 150 or 200 years ago. Approximately five hundred of such charburner plates are distributed across the national park.

A place of cultural-historic importance is the former Quernstkirche between Altenlotheim and Frebershausen. The ground plan of the House of God, which was mentioned in writing for the first time in 1230, can only be vaguely discerned from the flat overgrown walls. After the reformation, it became more and more of a ruin and the stones were used for the construction of houses in Altenlotheim. The church was not as far afield as it seems today. The inhabitants of the neighbouring villages buried their dead in its graveyard. Every year on the 3rd of May, the Day of the Cross, a large carnival used to take place. The city of Frankenau built a chapel at this historic site in 2006. A place of prayer and awe, a possibility of being in still dialogue with nature.

It is owing to the hunting passion of previous generations that the wonderful meadow valleys in national park have been protected: The abbots of Haina and the princes of Waldeck used to hunt capital deer in these regions.

88 | AUF SPURENSUCHE – SICHTBARE GESCHICHTE

Wenig wissen wir über die Menschen der Bronzezeit, die vor 3.000 Jahren unter dem Schutz solcher Steinhügel ihre Toten bestatteten.

*We know only a little about the Bronze Age people who buried their dead protected by such stone mounds more than 3,000 years ago.*

Hohlwege: Über Jahrhunderte haben Ochsenkarren tiefe Spuren hinterlassen. Hier hat sich das Scharbockskraut angesiedelt.

*Narrow path: Oxen carts have left deep traces over the centuries. Here, the fig buttercup has settled.*

LOOKING FOR CLUES – VISIBLE HISTORY | 89

Die idyllische Bathildishütte gehörte zu einem Jagdhaus, benannt nach einer Waldeckischen Fürstin.

*The idyllic Bathildishütte (Bathildis hut) is part of the hunting lodge and named after a Waldeck princess.*

Erst aus der Vogelperspektive lassen sich die Umrisse der mittelalterlichen Quernstkirche erahnen.

*Only a bird's eye view reveals the vague outline of the medieval Quernstkirche.*

**Grenzsteine**
*Landmarks*

Fürstentum Waldeck links

Großherzogtum Hessen rechts

Im Volksmund: „Fette Wurst" und „Großer Hunger"

*Principality of Waldeck on the left*

*Grand duchy of Hessen on the right*

*In the vernacular: „Fatty sausage" and „Huge appetite"*

Von Wildschweinen an den Tag gebracht: alte Köhlerplatte mit Holzkohleresten

*Discovered by wild boars: old charburner plate with remnants of charcoal*

Heide auf dem Fahrentriesch – Zeugin uralter Kulturlandschaft

*Heath on the Fahrentriesch – witness of an ancient cultural landscape*

Schäferin Annette Flandorfer mit ihren schwarzköpfigen Rhönschafen auf dem Fahrentriesch

*The sheperdess Annette Flandorfer with her black-headed Rhönschafen (old German sheep species) on the Fahrentriesch*

Die landschaftsprägenden Waldwiesentäler im Nationalpark sind ökologisch sehr wertvoll.

*The forest glades shaping the landscape of the national park are of high ecological importance.*

Die alte Wolfsfalle am Ruhlauber bei Frebershausen ist auf einer historischen Karte belegt.

*The old wolf trap at Ruhlauber near Frebershausen is marked on a historic map.*

Kastanienbäume im Blütenschmuck – angepflanzt als Nahrungsspender für Rot- und Damwild

*Chestnut trees in full bloom – planted as a food source for red and fallow deer*

Herrliche Aussicht im Wildpark: Edersee mit Schloss und Stadt Waldeck

*Beautiful view in the wildlife park: Lake Eder with castle and the city of Waldeck*

# Edersee – ein „Fjord" im Kellerwald

*Natur Natur sein lassen – kein Thema, als 1908 bis 1914 die Edertalsperre entstand. Eines der schönsten Täler weit und breit versank in den Fluten des Stausees – und mit ihm die Orte Asel, Berich und Bringhausen.*

„Die Dörfer und Gehöfte waren nur über schmale Verbindungswege zu erreichen. Die Menschen lebten noch ihr eigenes Leben – in Ruhe und Beschaulichkeit. Nur der Klang der Kirchenglocken oder der Schuss des Jägers unterbrachen diese Stille. Wenn im Frühling das Grün der Wiesen und Saaten und die in Blüte stehenden Obstgärten von der Sonne überflutet wurden und die Eder wie ein leuchtendes Band das Tal durchzog, dann glaubte man sich in eine verzauberte Welt versetzt." So schilderte der Heimatdichter Christian Kohl aus Hemfurth seine Erinnerungen an das versunkene Tal.

Wer heute im Frühjahr oder Sommer per Schiff den Edersee befährt, ihn mit dem Rad umrundet oder von der Terrasse der alten Grafenburg Waldeck aus bewundert, der ahnt freilich nichts von dieser Vergangenheit. Der zweitgrößte Stausee Deutschlands präsentiert sich in herrlichem Einklang mit der Natur: ein blaues Band, tief eingebettet in die Bergwelt des Kellerwaldes. Der Vergleich mit den wilden Fjorden des fernen Norwegens drängt sich auf.

Anders das Bild im Herbst! Nach und nach sinkt der Wasserstand, weil Stauraum als Schutz vor Hochwasser benötigt wird und der Edersee Wasser zur Aufrechterhaltung der Schifffahrt auf der Weser liefert. Ganz allmählich verändert dann der See sein Antlitz. Das alte Ederbett wird über viele Kilometer hinweg wieder sichtbar, die Fluten geben geheimnisvolle Spuren der Vergangenheit frei: die untergegangenen Dorfplätze, die gut erhaltene Sandsteinbrücke bei Asel-Süd oder das alte Mauerwerk der Bericher Hütte bei Nieder-Werbe, einst wichtigster Ort der Eisenindustrie im Waldecker Land.

Im oberen Bereich des Edersees entsteht Jahr für Jahr durch das Absenken des Wasserspiegels eine neue Wildnis, das „Wattenmeer" bei Herzhausen mit einer in Mitteleuropa einmaligen Tier- und Pflanzenwelt. Schritt für Schritt begrünen sich ab August die trockengefallenen Schlickflächen. Arten wie das Schlammkraut – die kleinste Blütenpflanze Deutschlands – bis hin zu Massenbeständen der kniehohen Schlanksegge, erobern den Seeboden. Hier präsentiert sich das größte zusammenhängende Seggenried Deutschlands. Man muss schon an Biebza oder Narew reisen, die großen Wildflüsse im Nordosten Polens, um so eindrucksvolle Lebensräume zu sehen.

# Lake Eder – a „fjord" in the Kellerwald

*Let nature be nature – nobody cared when the Lake Eder dam was built between 1908 and 1914. One of the most beautiful valleys far and wide was engulfed by the floodwaters of the dam – and with it the towns of Asel, Berich and Bringhausen.*

„The villages and homesteads could only be reached via narrow connecting paths. The people still lived their own lives – quietly and contemplatively. The silence was only disturbed by the chiming of the church bells or the hunter's shot. When the green of the meadows and the crops and the blooming orchards were flooded by the spring sunlight and the River Eder was flowing through the valley like a blue ribbon, it felt like being moved into an enchanted world." This is how the regional writer Christian Kohl of Hemfurth describes his memories of the sunken valley.

Today, if you go on a boat trip on Lake Eder or circle around it by bike or take an admiring look from the terrace of the old Waldeck castle in spring or summer, you will, of course, sense nothing of its past. The second largest dam in Germany presents itself in marvellous harmony with nature: its blue ribbon deeply embedded in the Kellerwald mountains. The comparison with the wild Norwegian fjords stands to reason.

But the picture in autumn is different! Gradually the water level falls since the reservoir is needed as protection against flood waters and Lake Eder provides water for the maintenance of shipping on the River Weser. Gradually, the lake changes its appearance. The old river bed becomes visible again for several kilometers, the floods uncover mysterious traces of the past: sunken village squares, the well-preserved sandstone bridge near Asel-Süd or the old walls of the Bericher Hütte (Bericher hut) near Nieder-Werbe, once the most important town of the iron industry in the county of Waldeck.

Year after year, a new wilderness is developing in the upper region of Lake Eder due to the lowering of the water level: the „wadden sea" near Herzhausen with flora and fauna unique in central Europe. Beginning in August, the dried up slush areas gradually become green. The bottom of the lake is conquered by species ranging from the water mudwort – the smallest flowering plant in Germany – to the mass population of the knee-high slender spiked sedge. Here Germany's largest cohesive sedge reed presents itself. Normally you'd have to travel as far as the big, wild rivers of Biebza and Narew in the northeast of Poland to find such impressive habitats.

Blauer „Fjord" im Kellerwald

*Blue "fjord" in the Kellerwald*

Eindrucksvolles Schauspiel im Frühjahr: Die Sperrmauer läuft über!

*Impressive spectacle in spring: The dam wall is flooded!*

Mit der weißen Flotte den Nationalpark genießen

*Enjoying the national park with the white fleet*

Edersee – eng umschlungen vom Buchenmeer

*Lake Eder – closely entwined by a sea of beeches*

Bei Niedrigwasser entsteht es Jahr für Jahr wieder: das alte Ederbett.

*Year after year it emerges again at low water: the old bed of the river Eder.*

Nebelschleier über dem Edersee an der geheimnisvollen Hünselburg – ein Ort aus keltischer Zeit?

*Veils of fog above Lake Eder at the mystic Hünselburg – a place from Celtic times?*

Banfemündung
im Nebel

*Mouth of the Banfe
in fog*

Die Wooghölle als
Spiegelbild

*The Wooghölle
as a reflection*

Die Burg am Wald-Eck – einst Stammsitz der Waldecker Grafen

*The castle at Wald-Eck – once the ancestral seat of the dukes of Waldeck*

Spurensuche im Edersee: Alt-Bringhausen gibt seine Geheimnisse preis.

*Looking for clues in Lake Eder: Alt-Bringhausen discloses its secrets.*

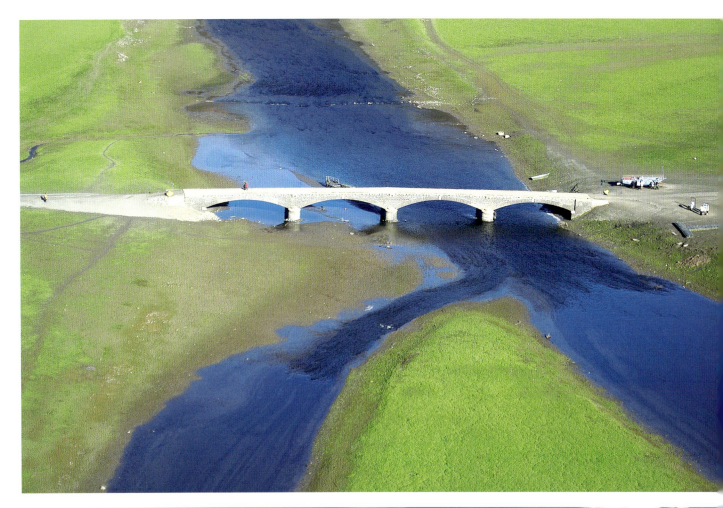

Aufgetaucht aus den Fluten: die alte Sandstein-Brücke bei Asel

*Reemerged from the depths: the old sandstone bridge near Asel*

Alljährlich bildet es sich neu: das ausgedehnte Seggenried bei Herzhausen. Im Vordergrund Gilbweiderich

*Every year it crops up again: the expansive sedge reed near Herzhausen. Loosestrife in foreground*

104 | EDERSEE – EIN „FJORD" IM KELLERWALD

Sinfonie von Wolken, Wald und Wasser

*Symphony of clouds, woods and water*

„Wattenmeer" am Edersee

*„Wadden sea" on Lake Eder*

Schöne Einblicke in die Kinderstube des Haubentauchers bietet eine der größten hessischen Kolonien bei Herzhausen.

*Lovely insights in the nursery of the great crested grebe are offered by one of largest Hessian colonies near Herzhausen.*

Nach 35 Jahren brütet der Wanderfalke wieder am Edersee.

*The peregrine breeds at Lake Eder again after 35 years.*

Goldener Oktobertag am Edersee

*Golden days of October at Lake Eder*

Verständigung auf „Wisentisch"

*Communication in „bison language"*

# Bei Uhu, Wolf und Otter – ein Besuch im Wildpark

*Im Wildpark, einer Einrichtung des Nationalparks, sind Tiere zu bestaunen, die im Kellerwald heimisch sind oder es früher einmal waren. Wildkatze oder Luchs könnten im Nationalpark wieder Lebensraum finden.*

Wir haben unseren Familienausflug in den Wildpark Edersee zeitlich so geplant, dass wir die nachmittägliche Flugschau der Greifenwarte erleben können. Das „Fagutop", eine sehenswerte Präsentation des Lebensraums Buchenwald im Eingangsbereich, wollen wir uns unbedingt auf dem Rückweg anschauen. Jetzt drängen die Kinder erst einmal zu den Tieren. Im Wildschwein-Gehege entdecken wir eine Bache mit braun-gelb gestreiften Frischlingen. Dann begegnen wir zutraulichen Damhirschen, die Futter aus der Hand nehmen. Vorsicht, sonst ist gleich die ganze Tüte weg!

Schon viele Menschen – Alt und Jung – warten auf die Flugschau. Ein großartiger Blick: der Edersee und drüben die Burg Waldeck. Und dann die eleganten Flugspiele der Adler und Falken! Köpfe einziehen, ein Geier gleitet dicht über uns. Am Schluss den Uhu streicheln! Die beiden Falkner erzählen viel Interessantes über die gefiederten Jäger und die uralte Kunst, mit Vögeln zu jagen. Wir erfahren, dass Rot- und Schwarzmilan sowie Uhu im Nationalpark brüten und der Wanderfalke unweit des Nationalparks seine Jungen aufzieht. Seit einigen Jahren erscheint regelmäßig ein freilebender Schwarzmilan zur Flugschau und holt sich Nahrungsbrocken als Belohnung ab.

Weiter geht es zum Luchsgehege. Ob wohl die eindrucksvollen Großkatzen mit den Pinselohren wieder bei uns heimisch werden? Voller Geheimnisse erscheint das Wolfsrudel, nach dem wir länger Ausschau halten müssen. Der letzte Wolf im Waldecker Land wurde 1819 / 20 bei Freienhagen erlegt.

Die eindrucksvollste Wildart, der wir im Nationalpark in freier Wildbahn begegnen können, ist der Rothirsch. Es gehört schon ein wenig Glück dazu, seine urigen Schreie im Herbstwald zu vernehmen. Will man die Hirschbrunft erleben, ist der Wildpark Anfang September ein guter Tipp. Der „König der Wälder" lebt hier in einem großen Gehege, das landschaftlich reizvoll hoch über dem Edersee liegt.

Vorbei an Wildpferd, Wisent und Auerhahn eilen wir zum Gehege der Fischotter, weil wir die Fütterung beobachten wollen. Schon nähert sich der Tierpfleger mit einem Eimer voll Fische. Ob die beiden Otter wohl aus ihren Verstecken kommen? Ja, sie kennen ihre Fütterungszeiten, gleiten rasch ins Wasser und jagen pfeilschnell die quirligen Fische. Welch elegante Schwimmer diese Wassermarder doch sind. Noch im 19. Jahrhundert waren an der Eder Otter durchaus keine Seltenheit. Der letzte wurde 1911 bei Bergheim geschossen.

Nach dem Rundgang nehmen wir uns noch Zeit für die Erkundung des Fagutops. Auch die Kinder können hier auf vielfältige Weise und spielerisch den Lebensraum Buchenwald erkunden. Dann lockt sie der Spielplatz am Ausgang des Wildparks und eine Erfrischung in der „Bericher Hütte". Ein gelungener Nachmittag!

# With eurasian eagle owl, wolf and otter – a visit to the wildlife park

*In the wildlife park, an institution of the national park, animals which live or used to live in the Kellerwald can be marvelled at. The national park could become the habitat of the wildcat or the lynx again.*

We timed our family outing to the Lake Eder wildlife park so that we could experience the afternoon flight show at the bird of prey station. On our way back, we don't want to miss the „Fagutop", a presentation of the beech forest habitat in the foyer which is well worth seeing. But now the children are urging us to go see the animals. In the wild boar park we spot a wild sow with yellow-brown striped shoats. Then we encounter trusting fallow deers feeding from our hands. Careful or they will eat the whole goody bag!

Many people – young and old – are already waiting for the flight show to begin. A marvellous view: Lake Eder and Waldeck castle on the other side. And look at the elegant flight exercises of the eagles and falcons! Mind your head, a vulture sails right above us. Finally, let's pet the eurasian eagle owl! The two falconers tell interesting stories about the feathered hunters and the ancient art of hunting with birds. We learn that red and black kite as well as eurasian eagle owl brood in the national park, and that the peregrine raises its young in the immediate proximity of the national park. For some years now, a free-living black kite has regularly appeared at the flight show and comes for hunks of food as a reward.

Next stop is the lynx enclosure. Will these impressive big cats with the brush on the tip of their ears become domesticated again? The pack of wolves, for which we have to be on the look-out for quite a while, seems to be full of secrets. The last wolf in Waldeck county was killed near Freienhagen in 1819 / 1820.

The most impressive species of game which we can encounter in the wild in the national park is the red deer. It takes a little luck to hear its strange cries in the autumnal forest. If you want to experience the rutting season, come to the park at the beginning of September. The „King of the Woods" lives here in an extensive park situated high above Lake Eder in an attractive landscape.

Passing by wild horses, European bison and mountain cock, we hurry to the enclosure of the fish otter to watch the feeding. There comes the keeper carrying a bucket full of fish. Will the two otters leave their hiding place? Look, they know their feeding times, glide quickly into the water and hunt the lively fish, shooting fast as arrows. Very elegant swimmers, these sea martens! Still in the 19th century, otter were no rarity on the river Eder. The last was shot near Bergheim in 1911.

After the tour, we spend some time exploring the Fagutop. Children, too, can explore the beech forest habitat in many different and playful ways. Then their attention is drawn to the playground near the exit of the wildlife park and refreshments in the „Bericher Hütte". A successful afternoon!

112 | BEI UHU, WOLF UND OTTER – EIN BESUCH IM WILDPARK

Oh, sind die süß!

*How cute!*

Wildpark Edersee – ein Erlebnis für die ganze Familie

*Lake Eder wildlife park – an adventure for the whole family*

Wir durften den Uhu streicheln.

*We could pet the eurasian eagle owl.*

Einmal Falkner sein

*To be a falconer once in your life*

Kopf einziehen! Gänsegeier im Tiefflug

*Mind your head! Low flying eurasian griffon vulture*

Idylle bei Familie Luchs

*Lynx family idyll*

WITH EURASIAN EAGLE OWL, WOLF AND OTTER – A VISIT TO THE WILDLIFE PARK

Flinker Kletterkünstler Waschbär – Neubürger am Edersee seit 1934

*The racoon – agile climbing artist – new citizen on Lake Eder since 1934*

Star im Wildpark: Otterdame Jule

*The star of the wildlife park: otter lady Jule*

Uriger Brunftschrei am Edersee

*Strange rutting call on Lake Eder*

Geheimnisvoll und sagenumwoben – der Wolf

*Mysterious and legendary – the wolf*

Talgang und Quernstgrund bei Frebershausen – zwei Wege zu einem Ziel

*Talgang and Quernstgrund near Frebershausen – two paths to the same destination*

# Wege in den Nationalpark
# Routes into the national park

Mit dem „Wacholdermännchen" zum Heideblütenfest nach Altenlotheim

*Following the „Juniper manikin" to the Heath Blossom Carnival in Altenlotheim*

Welches ist der schönste Weg?

*Which is the most beautiful trail?*

Nationalparkdorf Kleinern im schönen Wesetal

*National park village of Kleinern in the beautiful Wesetal*

Frebershausen – dörfliche Idylle am Nationalpark

*Frebershausen – village idyll in the proximity of the national park*

Im schönsten
Wiesengrunde:
Quernstgrund bei
Frebershausen

*On the most beautiful
meadow grounds:
Quernstgrund near
Frebershausen*

Mit dem Ranger
unterwegs:
eingetaucht in
Wildnis

*On route with the
ranger:
submerged in
wilderness*

Walderlebnis mit allen Sinnen

*Experience the forest with all of your senses*

Mit zwei PS ins Reich der urigen Buchen

*With two horse power into the kingdom of quaint beeches*

Mit der Standseilbahn auf den Peterskopf bei Hemfurth – ein idealer Ausgangspunkt für Wanderungen

*Taking the cable car to the top of the Peterskopf near Hemfurth – an ideal starting point for hiking tours*

Den Urwaldsteig erkunden

*Exploring the Urwaldsteig*

Unvergessliche Erlebnisse bietet der Urwaldsteig

*The Urwaldsteig offers unforgettable adventures*

Frühling am Gutshof Asel-Süd

*Spring at the Asel-Süd estate*

So präsentiert sich vom Hagenstein aus das Edertal bei Kirchlotheim.

*This is how the Eder valley presents itself near Kirchlotheim viewed from the top of the Hagenstein.*

Ein Jahrhunderte alter Eichenbaum — An oak tree, centuries old
– im Zeitenwandel nur ein kurzer Traum. — – only a short dream through the ages.
Tausend Sterne ziehen ihre Bahnen, — A thousand stars follow their course,
lassen uns die Ewigkeit erahnen. — giving us a vague notion of eternity.
Tausend Bäume wachsen und vergehen, — A thousand trees grow and decay,
werden noch all diese Sterne sehen. — will still see all these stars.

# Kurzinformationen / Short informations

*Anmerkungen für fotografisch interessierte Leser*

Die überwiegende Anzahl der Bilder wurde mit der Digitalkamera Nikon D2X aufgenommen. Einige Bilder entstanden mit den Analogkameras Nikon F4 und F5. Für die Panoramabilder wurde die Hasselblad Xpan Kamera verwandt. Filmmaterial: Fuji Velvia 50ASA. Zum Einsatz kamen Nikon Objektive von 12 bis 600 mm und immer ein Stativ.
Alle Landschafts- und Pflanzenbilder sowie die Mehrzahl der Tierbilder wurden im Nationalpark und in der Ederseeregion aufgenommen. Einige wenige Tierbilder entstanden aus Naturschutzgründen im Wildpark.

*Notes for readers interested in photography*

The majority of the pictures were taken with the digital camera Nikon D2X. Some pictures were taken with the analogous cameras Nikon F4 and F5. The panorama pictures were taken with the Hasselblad Xpan. Film material: Fuji Velvia 50ASA. Nikon lenses between 12 and 600 mm and a tripod were always used.
All pictures of landscapes and plants as well as the majority of animal pictures were taken in the national park and in the Lake Eder region. Very view pictures were taken in the wildlife park for reasons of nature protection.

*Wichtige Adressen*

**Nationalparkamt Kellerwald-Edersee**
Laustraße 8, 34537 Bad Wildungen
Telefon: 0049. (0) 5621 75249-0
info@nationalpark-kellerwald-edersee.de
www.nationalpark-kellerwald-edersee.de

**Naturpark Kellerwald-Edersee**
Laustrasse 8, 34537 Bad Wildungen
Telefon: 0049. (0) 5621 96946-0
info@naturpark-kellerwald-edersee.de
www.naturpark-ke.de

**Kellerwaldverein e. V.**
Laustrasse 8, 34537 Bad Wildungen
Telefon: 0049. (0) 5621 96946-20
info@kellerwaldverein.de
www.kellerwaldverein.de

**Förderverein für den Nationalpark Kellerwald-Edersee e. V.**
Kellerwaldstraße 20, 34537 Bad Wildungen

*Einrichtungen des Nationalparks*

**Nationalparkhaus**
An einer der Haupteingangsrouten zum Nationalpark an der B 252 zwischen Herzhausen und Kirchlotheim entsteht ein Besucher- und Informationszentrum.

**Fagutop**
Das Informationszentrum über den Lebensraum Buchenwald ist dem Wildpark Edersee angegliedert.
Öffnungszeiten: siehe Wildpark
Telefon: 0049. (0) 5623 4370

**Wildpark Edersee**
Der Wildpark Edersee ist von dem Edertaler Ortsteil Hemfurth-Edersee aus (in Richtung Bringhausen) zu erreichen.

Öffnungszeiten:
01.05. – 31.10.:   9.00 – 18.00 Uhr
01.11. – 28.02.:  11.00 – 16.00 Uhr
01.03. – 30.04.:  10.00 – 18.00 Uhr
Telefon: 0049. (0) 5623 4370
Flugvorführungen der Greifenwarte vom 01.03. – 15.11. täglich außer montags 11.00 und 15.00 Uhr
Fütterungen der Greifenwarte vom 16.11. – 28.02. täglich außer montags 14.00 Uhr
Telefon: 0049. (0) 5623 2230

**Waldschule im Fagutop**
Angebote: siehe Veranstaltungskalender, Gruppen und Schulklassen können Termine über die Nationalparkverwaltung vereinbaren.

*Weiterführende Literatur*

**Bildband Naturpark und Nationalpark Kellerwald-Edersee**
H. Hücker und G. Kalden
cognitio Verlag ♦ ISBN 3-932583-12-4

**Bildband Naturerbe Kellerwald**
A. Frede, A. Hoffmann, R. Kubosch, N. Panek
cognitio Verlag ♦ ISBN 978-3-932583-22-3

**Bildband Urwaldsteig Edersee**
cognitio Verlag ♦ ISBN 978-3-932583-19-3

**Wanderführer Urwaldsteig Edersee**
cognitio Verlag ♦ ISBN 3-932583-14-0

**Natur- und Kulturführer Kellerwald-Edersee** von N. Panek
cognitio Verlag ♦ ISBN 978-3-932583-21-6